# THE World Series

DISCARD

## BASEBALL'S BIGGEST STAGE

## MATT DOEDEN

MILLBROOK PRESS · MINNEAPOLIS

Millbrook Press
A division of Lerner Publishing Group, Inc.
241 First Avenue North
Minneapolis, MN 55401 USA

For reading levels and more information, look up this title at www.lernerbooks.com.


Library of Congress Cataloging-in-Publication Data

Doeden, Matt
    The World Series : baseball's biggest stage / by Matt Doeden.
       pages   cm. — (Spectacular sports)
    Includes index.
    ISBN 978–1–4677–1896–7 (lib. bdg. : alk. paper)
    ISBN 978–1–4677–2543–9 (eBook)
    1. World Series (Baseball)—History—Juvenile literature.  I. Title.
  GV878.4.D64  2014
  796.357'646—dc23                              2013018082

Manufactured in the United States of America
1 – VI – 12/31/13

# CONTENTS

# INTRODUCTION
## PLAY BALL!

The stadium lights are shining. The sellout crowd is on its feet. The cameras are rolling. The umpire calls "Play ball!" into the crisp October air. It's the fantasy of every young baseball fan: the World Series. The chance for a championship and baseball immortality.

The World Series is called the Fall Classic for a reason. Among the major team sports, no championship has a more storied past. Hockey may have the most famous trophy in the Stanley Cup, while the Super Bowl might have the glitz and glamour. But when it comes to history and tradition, nothing can match the World Series. Since it started in 1903, it has provided baseball fans with measures of drama, scandal, inspiration, triumph, and heartbreak.

*Opposite page:* The St. Louis Cardinals celebrate their Game 7 World Series win at Busch Stadium in 2011.

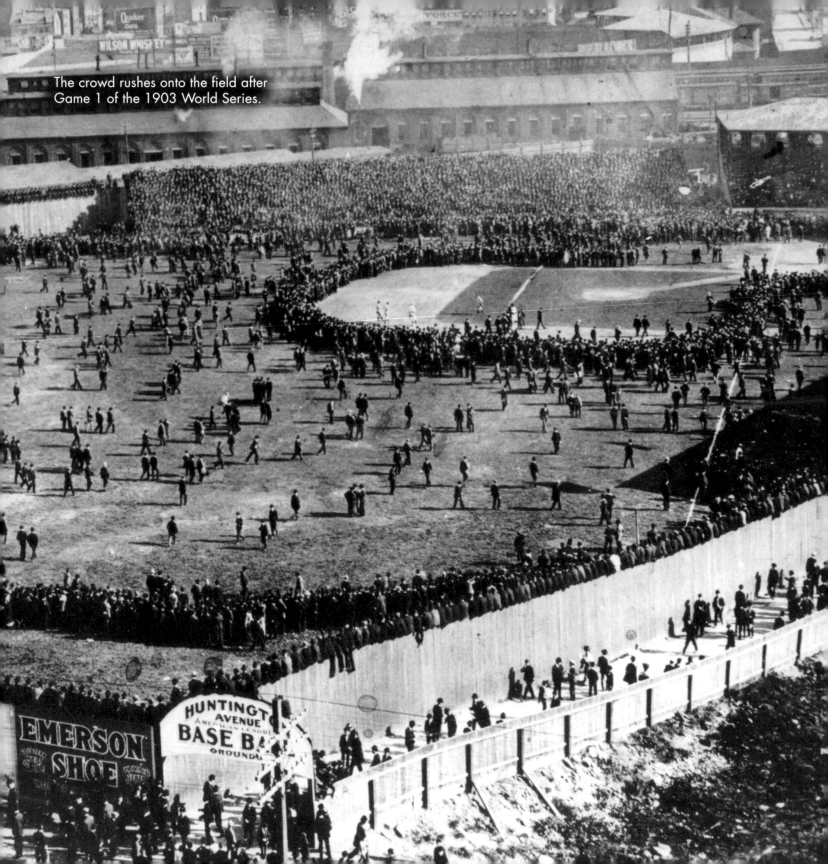

The crowd rushes onto the field after
Game 1 of the 1903 World Series.

# WORLD SERIES HISTORY

## A CENTURY OF THE FALL CLASSIC

The World Series may be a spectacle in recent years, but it didn't start out that way. In 1900 the National League (NL) was the dominant professional baseball league. But not every team was making money. So the NL decided to cut back from 12 teams to eight. Ban Johnson was the president of a small league called the Western League. He saw an opportunity to compete with the NL as a top league. Johnson created the American League (AL) and raided the NL for some of its best players.

Tensions between the two leagues were high. At first, NL owners had little interest in a series between the two leagues' champions. But that changed in 1903. The NL champion Pittsburgh Pirates challenged the AL champs, the Boston Americans (also called the Pilgrims or Patriots), to a series to determine the world championship. The clubs agreed to play a best-of-nine games series. And so the World Series was born. And what a series it was. The Pirates, favored to win it all, surged to a 3–1 series lead. But the Americans stormed back to win the next four games and stun the Pirates. If there was any question that the young AL was a match for the established NL, it was erased in that first series.

## THE FIRST WORLD SERIES?

Most historians view the 1903 World Series as the first. But some point to a series played in 1884. The New York Metropolitans, champions of a league called the American Association (AA), challenged the NL-champion Providence Grays to a championship series. They played three games in late October, in cold, windy conditions. Cold and darkness forced an early end to Game 2. Then the teams agreed to end Game 3 early because of darkness. The Grays won all three games and claimed the title of US champions.

The 1903 World Series was not a formal championship between the NL and the AL. League officials had not organized it. The Pirates and the Americans had arranged the series on their own. So in 1904, when the New York Giants won the NL title, they refused to play against Boston, the AL champs. The Giants claimed that the AL was an inferior league, despite the Americans' victory in the 1903 series. The Giants declared themselves world champs, and there was no World Series. It would be another 90 years before another fall without the Fall Classic.

## THE SERIES RETURNS

By 1905 the relationship between the two leagues had improved. Owners on both sides saw the advantages of a championship series. So they made it formal—the two champions would play a best-of-seven series in October. The first team to get four wins would take the championship. This format remains in place today.

The Giants won the NL again in 1905. This time, they were ready to face the AL champion Philadelphia Athletics. The Giants had described the AL as inferior, and they made their case in 1905 with an easy victory in five games. The NL looked to continue that dominance in 1906 with the Chicago Cubs, who went 116–36 during the regular season. But the Chicago White Sox stunned them in six games, bringing glory back to the AL. The Cubs bounced back and became the first back-to-back champs in 1907 and 1908. Modern baseball fans might find that ironic, since the Cubs haven't won the series since.

The early 1900s was an era of dynasties. The Philadelphia Athletics won it all in 1910, 1911, and 1913. Then the Boston Red Sox (formerly the Americans) took over, winning in 1915, 1916, and 1918. One of Boston's key players was a young pitcher named Babe Ruth. In three World Series starts, Ruth went 3–0 with a 0.87 earned run average (ERA). Those were outstanding numbers, but compared to Ruth's amazing hitting feats in years to come, they're all but forgotten.

This team postcard shows the 1915 Boston Red Sox. Pitcher Babe Ruth is in the top row of players, sixth from the left.

Pro baseball was thriving. The World Series was becoming a spectacle. Fans loved it. Owners and players liked the extra revenue it brought in. But change was on its way.

## DARK DAYS AND A NEW ERA

The 1919 season was one of change for baseball and the World Series, both for good and bad. First, it marked the beginning of an offensive explosion. Scoring soared league-wide, ending what historians call the Deadball Era. Secondly, it marked Ruth's final year in Boston. The Red Sox sold him to the New York Yankees after the season. And finally, that season's World Series still stands as perhaps the game's darkest days.

## THE DEADBALL ERA

Baseball historians refer to the period from 1900 to 1919 as the Deadball Era. During this time, offenses struggled to score runs. Home runs were extremely rare. The low point of the era came in 1908. That season, teams averaged just 3.4 runs per game, the lowest total in the game's modern era (1901–present day).

The 1919 season marked the end of the Deadball Era. Babe Ruth hit 29 home runs that season. Offense increased sharply. Historians don't agree on the exact reason for the sudden change. Some say it's because the ball itself changed. The old balls were softer. They were reused again and again, leading to flat spots that further deadened them off the bat. Others point to the building of smaller ballparks with shorter outfield fences. Still others say that outlawing the spitball, a pitch in which the pitcher actually used saliva or another substance to affect the ball's movement, gave offenses a huge boost. It was probably a combination of all these factors. One thing is certain—fans loved all the extra action. The end of the Dead Ball Era marked the beginning of a golden age of baseball that featured stars from Babe Ruth to Joe DiMaggio to Stan Musial.

The 1919 World Series between the Chicago White Sox and the Cincinnati Reds marked the beginning of a short-lived experiment to make the World Series a best-of-nine affair (it returned to its best-of-seven format three years later). The Reds won the series, 5–3. But that was not the headline. Eight Chicago players took money from gamblers to fix the series—to lose on purpose. The Black Sox scandal was an embarrassment to baseball and threatened to destroy fans' confidence that the games were being played fairly by both sides. Owners never wanted something like that to happen again. They

A number of newspapers ran this ad telling fans to "fix these faces in your memory" in 1920, after the Black Sox scandal the previous season.

appointed former judge Kenesaw Mountain Landis commissioner of baseball. After a lengthy investigation, in 1920 Landis handed down to the eight players the harshest punishment he could—banning them from the game for life.

Babe Ruth, by this time playing outfield for the Yankees, helped restore the reputation of baseball and the World Series. Ruth was tearing up the AL, hitting 54 home runs in 1920 and 59 the next season. Only a decade earlier, a dozen home runs could easily have led the league. Ruth's power was almost beyond imagination. Not surprisingly, fans loved it (with the possible exception of Red Sox fans, who watched their entire team hit just 17 home runs in 1921). Ruth led the Yankees to six World Series appearances during the 1920s and established the team as baseball's most prestigious franchise. His emergence as baseball's first true superstar, along with the strong, decisive actions of Commissioner Landis, helped baseball overcome what could have been a crippling scandal.

Yankee Joe DiMaggio takes a swing during the 1941 season.

The Yankee dynasty stretched on and on. Ruth retired, and outfielder Joe DiMaggio took over as the team's biggest star, followed by Mickey Mantle. From 1927 until 1962, the Yankees won 20 out of the 35 Fall Classics. It's a period of dominance that few teams in major sports have ever achieved.

## THE EXPANDING GAME

For 50 years, baseball had just 16 teams, all in the Northeast and the Midwest. But after the 1957 season, baseball finally expanded to the West Coast. The Brooklyn Dodgers and New York Giants each packed up and moved to California, becoming the Los Angeles Dodgers and the San Francisco Giants.

It didn't take long for the Fall Classic to follow them. On October 4, 1959, the Dodgers hosted the first World Series game on the West Coast. The Dodgers won the game 3–1 and went on to win the series. The Dodgers added two more world titles in 1963 and 1965.

Three games of the 1959 World Series were held at the Los Angeles Memorial Coliseum in California. Attendance at each game was more than 90,000.

By 1969 both leagues featured 12 teams. It was time for a change. The leagues were split into two divisions each—the East and the West. The champions of each division would face off in a League Championship Series (LCS). Then the winners of those series would meet in the World Series. It was a huge change. Baseball had always rewarded the teams with the best regular-season records. The change meant that an inferior team could get hot and edge out a team with a better record. Some hard-core fans hated it. But many more loved the added drama the extra playoff series provided.

## THE WILD CARD ERA

The format that featured two League Championship Series continued until 1994 (with the exception of an expanded playoff in the 1981 season, which had been shortened

## INTERNATIONAL PASTIME

Baseball has long been called the United States' national pastime. But with the addition of the Montreal Expos to the NL in 1969, it became truly international. The Toronto Blue Jays joined the AL in 1977. In 1992 the Blue Jays became the first Canadian team to win the World Series (and then they did it again in 1993).

The Blue Jays remain a big draw in Toronto, but the Expos constantly struggled to fill the stands. The team finally left Montreal after the 2004 season, moving to Washington, DC, and changing their name to the Nationals.

The Blue Jays play at the Rogers Centre in Toronto.

by a players' strike). In 1994 baseball planned to expand the playoffs once again, splitting each league into three divisions and adding a wild card—the team with the best record among non-division winners. But a players' strike ended the season early, and for the first time in 90 years, no World Series was played.

The expanded format finally played out on the field in 1995. A total of eight teams made the playoffs, with two divisional series preceding each LCS. Baseball traditionalists cried out against the change. They argued that luck played too large a factor in short playoff series and that the importance of the grueling 162-game schedule was being minimized. Some argued that a team that couldn't even win its own division shouldn't be able to hoist the World Series trophy. But that's exactly what happened two years later when the wild card Florida Marlins beat the Cleveland Indians in a thrilling seven-game World Series, scoring the series-clinching run in the bottom of the 11th inning!

Baseball added yet another wild card to each league in 2012, boosting the total number of playoff teams to 10. Under the new format, the two wild cards faced off in a one-game winner-take-all battle for the right to advance. Some baseball purists dislike the continually expanding playoffs. But the money these games bring in for both players and owners has trumped tradition, and expanded playoffs are unlikely to go away anytime soon.

Edgar Renteria of the Florida Marlins celebrates his World Series-winning single as he runs down the first base line in 1997.

# Other Baseball Championships

The World Series stands unchallenged as baseball's biggest stage. But what about other baseball championships, past and present? Read on to learn about a few others.

## COLLEGE WORLD SERIES

The top teams in US college baseball battle it out each year at the College World Series in Omaha, Nebraska. The series has been held since 1950, and the current format includes eight teams split into two divisions. The division champs face off in a best-of-three championship. The University of Southern California's 12 championships are the most of any school.

## WORLD BASEBALL CLASSIC

Since 2006 the biggest international baseball competition has been the World Baseball Classic. Every four years, 16 national teams compete for the gold medal—most of them stocked with at least some major-league players. Japan won the first two championships (2006 and 2009), with the Dominican Republic taking gold in 2013 *(below)*.

## NEGRO WORLD SERIES

The major leagues weren't the only high-end professional league during the first half of the 20th century. Black players, banned from the big leagues, turned instead to the Negro Leagues. The champs of the Negro American League and the Negro National League squared off in the Negro World Series from 1942 until 1948. The Homestead Grays won three of the seven series championships (1943, 1944, and 1948). The Negro Leagues slowly disbanded after Jackie Robinson became the major leagues' first black player in 1947.

## JAPAN SERIES

North Americans aren't the only ones who take their baseball seriously. The sport is every bit as big in Japan. Since 1950 the top Japanese teams have competed in the Japan Series, a best-of-seven competition. The Yomiuri Giants have claimed 22 championships, the most in series history.

## ALL-AMERICAN GIRLS PROFESSIONAL BASEBALL LEAGUE CHAMPIONSHIP

From 1943 to 1954, men weren't the only pro baseball players. The Midwest-based All-American Girls Professional Baseball League (AAGPBL) featured women's teams battling for their own championship. The Rockford Peaches of Rockford, Illinois, were the most successful team, winning AAGPBL titles in 1945, 1948, 1949, and 1950.

Dorothy Kamenshek played for the Rockford Peaches from 1943 to 1951 and in 1953.

# 2 UNFORGETTABLE
## THE GREATEST WORLD SERIES GAMES EVER PLAYED

Since the Fall Classic began in 1903, AL and NL teams have clashed in more than 600 World Series games. With a few exceptions, most have been filled with tension and drama, and most have had their moments of greatness. But a few games throughout history really stand out. They're the hard-fought games that featured two teams giving everything they had for the title of World Champion. They're the games that had fans talking not for a day or a week but for a lifetime. Each one stands as one of the greatest baseball games ever played.

### FINALLY!
### 1924, Game 7, Giants vs. Senators

Entering the 1924 season, future Hall of Fame pitcher Walter Johnson was 36 and nearing the end of his career. He'd never made a World Series. But that changed when he and the Washington Senators won the AL and earned a World Series date with the New York Giants.

Johnson's long-awaited World Series debut didn't begin well. He was the losing pitcher in Games 1 and 5. Yet Washington fought on, forcing the series to a deciding Game 7. Having pitched in Game 5, Johnson was not ready to start the series finale. It looked as though the living legend would yet again be denied his first win in the World Series.

Walter Johnson pitches during the 1924 World Series. He was inducted into the Baseball Hall of Fame in 1936.

Washington fans looked on glumly as the Giants held a 3–1 lead in the eighth inning. But then the Senators loaded the bases with two outs. Bucky Harris, Washington's second baseman (and manager), stepped to the plate. He hit a ground ball toward third baseman Freddie Lindstrom. It looked like an easy out, but the ball took a bad bounce and Lindstrom couldn't make the play. Two runs scored. Tie game!

The Senators made a surprise move in the ninth by bringing Johnson into the game as a reliever. The Giants threatened with two base runners, but Johnson got out of the jam. The Giants threatened again in the 10th and the 11th innings, but Johnson got out of each inning unscathed.

The Senators had one out in the bottom of the 12th when Muddy Ruel hit a pop foul. Giants catcher Hank Gowdy threw off his catcher's mask and positioned himself to make the catch. But as Gowdy shuffled his feet, he caught his foot in the mask. The ball landed harmlessly, allowing Ruel to continue the plate appearance. It was a costly mistake—Ruel went on to double and then came in to score the winning run on another New York error. Johnson, credited as the winning pitcher, finally had a chance to celebrate a World Series title.

## THE GREATEST GAME EVER PLAYED
### 1960, Game 7, Yankees vs. Pirates

Not everyone agrees which World Series game was the greatest. But reporters at the time dubbed Game 7 of the 1960 World Series the Greatest Game Ever Played, and the title has stuck.

The NL champion Pirates were heavy underdogs to the Yankees, who had played in eight of the previous 10 Fall Classics. New York's lineup was stocked with superstars and future Hall of Famers, while Pittsburgh's was filled with names unknown to many casual baseball fans. And indeed, on the whole, the Yankees seemed to dominate the series. Through six games, they had outscored the Pirates 46–17. Yet somehow, despite those lopsided numbers, the Pirates had managed to win three games and force a deciding Game 7.

The Pirates jumped out to an early lead, 4–0. Pittsburgh ace Vern Law did all he could to hold down the powerful Yankee lineup. But he was pitching on an injured ankle, and it was only a matter of time before the New York sluggers touched him up. The Yankees scored a run in the fifth, and when Law allowed two runners to reach base in the sixth, he was pulled for a reliever. The Yankees jumped all over the Pirates' thin bullpen. Yogi Berra hit a home run in a four-run inning. Then the Yankees added two more runs in the top of the eighth, silencing the Pittsburgh faithful.

The Pirates' hopes looked dim. With just six outs remaining, they were down 7–4. Worse still, they were facing Bobby Shantz, one of the best relievers in baseball. Gino Cimoli led off with a single. Then Bill Virdon hit a ground ball that looked like an easy double play. But the ball took a nasty hop and hit shortstop Tony Kubek in the throat. The runners were safe, and Kubek, with a mouthful of blood and a swollen windpipe, had to come out of the game.

The Pirates went on to score five runs that inning, highlighted by a pinch-hit, three-run home run from backup catcher Hal Smith. But again, they could not hold the lead. The Yankees scored twice in the top of the ninth to tie it again, 9–9.

Second baseman Bill Mazeroski stepped to the plate for the Pirates in the bottom of the ninth. Maz was known as a defensive wizard, but he wasn't much of an offensive threat and certainly not a slugger. Yankee pitcher Ralph Terry delivered a one-ball, no-strike pitch. Then Maz took a big swing. *Crack!* He launched the ball far over the left-field wall for a mammoth walk-off (game-ending) home run. The Pirates had pulled off the upset! The crowd erupted. Fans and players mobbed Mazeroski at home plate as he scored the winning run. It remains the only Game 7 walk-off home run in World Series history, and it was the most memorable moment of the Greatest Game Ever Played.

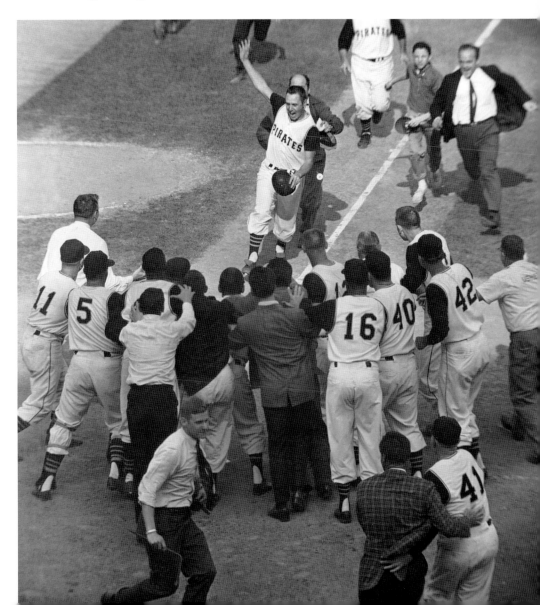

The Pittsburgh Pirates and fans wait for Bill Mazeroski *(center with hand raised)* to cross home plate after his home run won the 1960 World Series.

Since 1967 the World Series winners have received the Commissioner's Trophy, although it didn't officially bear that name until 1985. The sterling silver trophy stands 2 feet (0.6 meters) tall and weighs about 30 pounds (14 kilograms). It features one flag for each major-league team (currently 30) and the signature of the baseball commissioner at the bottom.

## LIVE TO FIGHT ANOTHER DAY
### 1975, Game 6, Reds vs. Red Sox

Few images are as vivid to baseball fans as the end of Game 6 of the 1975 series. The series featured the powerful Cincinnati Reds, nicknamed the Big Red Machine, facing off against a Boston Red Sox team that had entered the season with low expectations. Few fans had thought they'd win their division, much less the World Series.

The teams sat waiting for three days while rain poured down on Boston. Cincinnati led the series 3–2, so the Red Sox had to win or it was all over. Finally, the rain let up and the players took the field. The game that followed proved well worth the wait. Superstar outfielder Fred Lynn got the Red Sox off with a bang, clubbing a three-run homer in the first inning. But the Reds evened the score at 3–3 in the fifth. They added two more runs in the seventh and another in the eighth, giving them a 6–3 lead.

Boston put two runners on right away in the bottom of the eighth, but Reds' reliever Rawly Eastwick entered the game and got two quick outs. Pinch hitter Bernie Carbo stepped to the plate. Eastwick appeared to be in control, with Carbo taking feeble, awkward swings. But on a count of three balls, two strikes, Carbo finally got a good swing in. He crushed the ball over the center-field fence, bringing the crowd to its feet. Tie game!

Boston appeared to be in position to win it in the bottom of the ninth. They loaded the bases with no outs. Lynn hit a short fly ball to left fielder George Foster. The runner on third tried to tag up and score the winning run, but Foster's throw to the plate was strong and spot-on. The rally was squashed, the Reds got out of the inning, and the game went into extra innings.

Carlton Fisk waves the ball fair in Game 6 of the 1975 World Series.

In the top of the 11th, the Reds had a runner on first with second baseman Joe Morgan at the plate. Morgan drove the ball to deep left field. It looked like a sure extra-base hit. But left fielder Dwight Evans made a spectacular catch. He turned and fired the ball back to first base. The throw beat the runner to the bag for a double play.

Finally, in the 12th inning, Boston catcher Carlton Fisk stepped to the plate. On the second pitch he saw, Fisk lifted a long fly ball down the left-field line. It had the distance. The question was whether the ball would drift into foul territory. Fisk wildly waved his arms to the right, as if willing the ball to stay fair. It did, by inches, glancing off the foul pole. Home run! The camera shot of Fisk waving his arms remains one of the sport's iconic images.

It was a great moment for the Red Sox, but it was not, in the end, a happy ending. The Reds scored a ninth-inning run in Game 7 to earn a 4–3 victory and claim the World Series title. Still, many fans remember Game 6 as one of the greatest of all time.

## A FITTING FINISH
## 1991, Game 7, Braves vs. Twins

When it comes to classic World Series battles, few can compete with 1991. The Atlanta Braves and the Minnesota Twins fought it out in one close game after the next. Five of the seven games were decided by a single run. Four of them were decided on the final play. And three of them went to extra innings.

The Braves led the series three games to two, but the final two games were played in Minnesota's Metrodome. The Twins won an emotional Game 6 when superstar outfielder Kirby Puckett hit an extra-inning walk-off home run. In a series that had already reached legendary status, the best was yet to come.

Game 7 was a classic pitchers' duel, with 36-year-old Minnesota native Jack Morris battling Atlanta's young gun, John Smoltz. Both pitchers were brilliant. Scoring chances were few and far between in the early innings. It remained scoreless entering the eighth inning.

In the top of the eighth, Atlanta's Lonnie Smith stood on first base with one out. Terry Pendleton ripped a double to left-center field. Smith should have scored the game's first run easily. But Minnesota second baseman Chuck Knoblauch and shortstop Greg Gagne pretended that they were starting a double play. Smith was confused and hesitated. Instead of scoring, he was left standing at third. It was a costly mistake. Morris got out of the inning without allowing a run.

The Twins were next. They loaded the bases with one out. But first baseman Kent Hrbek hit a line drive right to an infielder. It was an easy double play. Again in the ninth, both teams had their chances, but neither could score. It was on to extra innings—the first winner-take-all extra-inning World Series game since the Senators beat the Giants in 1924!

Twins manager Tom Kelly was ready to take Morris out of the game. But the veteran pitcher refused. He went out and shut down the Braves in the top of the 10th. In the bottom of the inning, the Twins threatened again. Outfielder Dan Gladden hit a broken-bat pop fly that dropped in front of an outfielder. It looked like a single. But Gladden knew the ball would bounce high off the Metrodome turf. He tore around first base at top speed and dove into second base, just ahead of the tag. Knoblauch laid down a sacrifice bunt to move Gladden to third base.

The Braves intentionally walked Puckett, whose extra-inning heroics had forced Game 7 in the first place. Then they

Dan Gladden celebrates as he runs home to score the winning run of the 1991 World Series for the Twins.

chose to walk Hrbek as well. Although he had struggled in the series, Hrbek was a powerful fly ball hitter, and with Gladden's speed, any ball hit to the outfield would probably end it.

With the bases loaded, Kelly called on backup first baseman Gene Larkin to pinch hit. It was a risky move. Larkin had an injured knee and could barely run. If he hit the ball to an infielder, it would be a sure double play. But Larkin didn't do that. He smacked the first pitch over the heads of the Braves' outfielders. Gladden threw his arms into the air as he raced home for the winning run. The Twins stormed the field, winners of one of the most competitive World Series ever played.

## WALK-OFF WINNER
### 1993, Game 6, Phillies vs. Blue Jays

In 1993 the Blue Jays were looking to win their second straight title. They appeared in good shape to do so, jumping out to lead the series 3–1 over the NL champion

As expected, offense was sparse early on. The Diamondbacks finally got to Clemens in the sixth. Outfielder Danny Bautista lined an RBI double to left-center. Bautista was thrown out when he tried to stretch the hit to a triple, but Arizona was on the board.

New York struck back in the top of the seventh. With Derek Jeter on third base, first baseman Tino Martinez singled to right field to tie the game. Then Alfonso Soriano gave the Yankees the lead with a home run in the eighth inning. Arizona manager Bob Brenly made a surprise move later in the eighth, bringing Randy Johnson—the previous game's starter—in as a relief pitcher. Johnson got Arizona out of the inning and pitched a scoreless ninth as well.

The Diamondbacks trailed 2–1 with just three outs remaining. They were facing Yankee closer Mariano Rivera, probably the greatest relief pitcher of all time. But Arizona was up to the challenge. Mark Grace opened the inning by sending a single up the middle. Then Damian Miller attempted a sacrifice bunt. Rivera fielded the bunt, turned, and fired the ball to second base. His throw was wild, however, and both runners were safe.

Roger Clemens pitches during the first inning of Game 7 of the 2001 World Series.

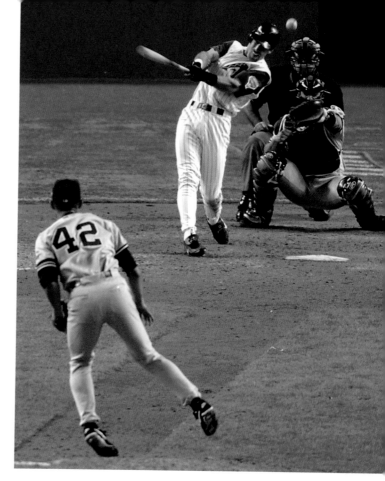

Luis Gonzalez hits a soft fly ball off Yankee closer Mariano Rivera to win the 2001 World Series.

Arizona tried another sacrifice bunt, but this time, Rivera threw out the runner at third. It appeared that third baseman Scott Brosius had a chance to complete a double play at first base, but he held the ball, leaving runners at first and second with one out.

The unlikely rally continued when Tony Womack laced a double to right field, tying the game at 2–2. The light-hitting Craig Counsell stepped up, but a pitch got away from Rivera and hit Counsell, loading the bases for slugger Luis Gonzalez. The Yankees brought their infield in, hoping to get a force out at home plate on a ground ball.

With the crowd on its feet, Rivera got strike one. His second pitch was on the inner part of the plate. Gonzalez didn't get a strong swing, but it was enough. He hit a soft fly over the head of the drawn-in Derek Jeter. As the ball hit the ground, Arizona's Jay Bell trotted home with the winning run. The Diamondbacks mobbed him at home plate as the fans went wild.

## NEVER SAY DIE
## 2011, Game 6, Rangers vs. Cardinals

The 2011 St. Louis Cardinals were one of the most unlikely World Series teams in history. On August 25, they trailed the Braves by a whopping 10.5 games for the NL

# 3 COMING UP CLUTCH
## THE BEST WORLD SERIES PERFORMERS

Some players just seem to shine on the biggest stage. Role players become superstars. Superstars become legends. In a series that can be decided in just four games, all it takes for a player to etch his name in baseball lore forever is a little hot streak. Which players have come up biggest on the big stage of the World Series? Let's take a look at a few shining stars.

## WORLD SERIES MVPs

Since 1955 baseball has singled out a Most Valuable Player of the World Series. The first World Series MVP was Johnny Podres of the Brooklyn Dodgers. The award traditionally goes to the most outstanding player on the winning team. But in 1960, the award went to Bobby Richardson, a member of the losing Yankees, after he set a series record with 12 RBIs. Three players have won the award two times: Sandy Koufax (1963 and 1965), Bob Gibson (1964 and 1967), and Reggie Jackson (1973 and 1977).

## YOGI BERRA

From 1947 to 1963, Hall of Fame catcher and outfielder Yogi Berra *(top right)* was a fixture in the World Series. He played in 14 series and won 10 championships (both records). Berra has the most plate appearances (295) in World Series history, as well as the most hits (71). His 12 home runs in the Fall Classic are the third most of all time. Berra never won a World Series MVP award, but that is partly because the honor didn't exist in 1953, his finest World Series performance, when he batted a torrid .429.

**World Series Stats**

| Games | Avg. | HR | RBI | R |
|---|---|---|---|---|
| 75 | .274 | 12 | 39 | 41 |

## WHITEY FORD

When it comes to starting pitchers, nobody enjoyed more success than Hall of Famer Whitey Ford. Ford played for the Yankees during their dynasty years of the 1950s and the early 1960s. That meant that the lefty got plenty of chances to play in the Fall Classic. Ford's 22 World Series starts and 146 innings pitched are both records, as are his 10 wins. His most amazing World Series feat was a 33-inning scoreless streak during his World Series appearances in 1960, 1961 *(bottom right)*, and 1962. He was the series MVP in 1961, winning both games he pitched without surrendering an earned run.

**World Series Stats**

| Games | Wins | Losses | ERA | Strikeouts |
|---|---|---|---|---|
| 22 | 10 | 8 | 2.71 | 94 |

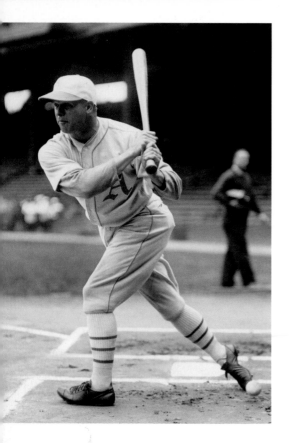

## JIMMIE FOXX

Jimmie Foxx *(top left)* of the Philadelphia Athletics was called the Right-Handed Babe Ruth for a reason—he could really slug the ball. Foxx appeared in three World Series: 1929, 1930, and 1931. He batted over .330 in each of them and led the Athletics to titles in 1929 and 1930.

**World Series Stats**

| Games | Avg. | HR | RBI | R |
|---|---|---|---|---|
| 18 | .344 | 4 | 11 | 11 |

## LOU GEHRIG

Babe Ruth often gets the credit for being the force that drove the powerhouse Yankees of the 1920s and the early 1930s. But in the World Series, Gehrig might have been even better. The Iron Horse played in seven World Series, winning all but the first of them. His 1928 series remains a legend. Gehrig batted .545 and hit four homers in just four games. Then, in 1932, he almost duplicated that feat, batting .529 with three home runs.

**World Series Stats**

| Games | Avg. | HR | RBI | R |
|---|---|---|---|---|
| 34 | .361 | 10 | 35 | 30 |

Lou Gehrig *(second from right)* follows Babe Ruth *(center)* across home plate after hitting a home run in the 1932 World Series.

## BOB GIBSON

Two-time World Series MVP Bob Gibson was at his best during the Fall Classic. Gibson was a classic strikeout pitcher who could blow hitters away. He led the Cardinals to the World Series in 1964, 1967, and 1968, bringing home the title in the first two of those years. His best series was 1967 *(right)*. Gibson went 3–0 with a 1.00 ERA. Although the Cards lost the 1968 World Series, Gibson turned in a record-breaking performance, striking out 17 hitters in Game 1.

**World Series Stats**

| Games | Wins | Losses | ERA | Strikeouts |
|---|---|---|---|---|
| 9 | 7 | 2 | 1.89 | 92 |

## LEFTY GOMEZ

Pitching for the Yankees of the 1930s gave Lefty Gomez a head start on World Series heroics. He appeared in five World Series, and New York won all five. Gomez compiled a perfect 6–0 World Series record. No other pitcher has won as many World Series games without a loss.

**World Series Stats**

| Games | Wins | Losses | ERA | Strikeouts |
|---|---|---|---|---|
| 7 | 6 | 0 | 2.86 | 31 |

## REGGIE JACKSON

Slugger Reggie Jackson was so good during his five trips to the World Series that he earned the nickname Mr. October. He was already a World Series hero, having

Jackson swats the ball during the 1973 World Series.

led the Oakland A's to two titles, when he signed with the Yankees in 1977. He helped the Yankees reach the Fall Classic, and then he turned in one of the greatest hitting performances in World Series history. In six games, Jackson hit five home runs, including a record three in Game 6.

**World Series Stats**

| Games | Avg. | HR | RBI | R |
|---|---|---|---|---|
| 27 | .357 | 10 | 24 | 21 |

### SANDY KOUFAX

Starting pitcher Sandy Koufax *(left, in the 1965 World Series)* may have been the most dominating pitcher ever to take the mound. Koufax struggled during his early years with the Dodgers. But something changed in 1961. Koufax learned to combine his raw power with precise control, and he became virtually unhittable. Fans and fellow players nicknamed him the Left Arm of God.

Koufax started seven games over four World Series. He posted a jaw-dropping ERA of 0.95 and struck out more than one batter per inning. He went 2–0 in the 1963 series and again in 1965. He was named MVP of both series. Injury limited him to just one start in the 1966 championship. Koufax retired after the Dodgers lost the series to the Baltimore Orioles. He was just 30 years old.

**World Series Stats**

| Games | Wins | Losses | ERA | Strikeouts |
|-------|------|--------|------|------------|
| 8 | 4 | 3 | 0.95 | 61 |

## MICKEY MANTLE

Mickey Mantle *(top right, during the 1960 World Series)* didn't hit for a high average in the World Series. But when it comes to home runs, no one can match him. The Mick hit a World Series record 18 homers in 12 series appearances. His best series, ironically, came in 1960, when the Yankees lost to the Pirates. Mantle batted .400 with three home runs and 11 RBIs.

**World Series Stats**

| Games | Avg. | HR | RBI | R |
|-------|------|-----|-----|-----|
| 65 | .257 | 18 | 40 | 42 |

## CHRISTY MATHEWSON

No pitcher has ever dominated a series the way Hall of Famer Christy Mathewson *(right)* did for the New York Giants in 1905, when they became World Champions. Mathewson took the mound in Game 1 and threw a shutout against the Philadelphia Athletics. He allowed just four hits during the game. Three days later, he started Game 3 and did it again. And two days after that, Mathewson started Game 5. On only one day of rest, Mathewson must have been tired—this time, he allowed five hits while hurling his third shutout in a week! Mathewson and the Giants returned to the series in 1911, 1912, and 1913. While Mathewson pitched well, the Giants lost all three.

**World Series Stats**

| Games | Wins | Losses | ERA | Strikeouts |
|-------|------|--------|------|------------|
| 11 | 5 | 5 | 0.97 | 48 |

## PAUL MOLITOR

Infielder Paul Molitor *(below, in the 1993 World Series)* only got to play in two World Series in his brilliant 21-year career. But when he got there, he really shined. Molitor had

a great series with the Milwaukee Brewers in 1982, batting .355 and scoring 5 runs, but the Brewers lost to the Cardinals. Then, 11 years later, at the age of 37, Molitor was back in the World Series with the Blue Jays. This time, he would not be denied. Molitor got 12 hits in 24 at bats during the series, batting an amazing .500! He also blasted two home runs and scored 10 times. It's a performance few have ever matched, making Molitor an easy choice for series MVP that year.

**World Series Stats**

| Games | Avg. | HR | RBI | R |
|-------|------|------|-----|-----|
| 13 | .418 | 2 | 11 | 15 |

## JACK MORRIS

Morris's iconic 10-inning shutout of the Atlanta Braves in the 1991 World Series remains one of the greatest pitching performances of all time. But Morris's World Series résumé doesn't end there. He played in three World Series, for three different franchises, and won all three. In 1984 he led the Detroit Tigers to the World Series, where he went 2–0 with a 2.00 ERA. Morris was the 1991 World Series MVP *(top right)*, going 2–0 for the Minnesota Twins and posting a 1.17 ERA. He was unable to reproduce that success in 1992 with the Blue Jays, but he still collected a third championship ring as the Jays defeated the Braves.

**World Series Stats**

| Games | Wins | Losses | ERA | Strikeouts |
|-------|------|--------|------|-----------|
| 7 | 4 | 2 | 2.96 | 40 |

## MARIANO RIVERA

With a record 11 career World Series saves, Mariano Rivera *(bottom right, in Game 4 of the 1999 World Series)* may be the greatest closer in World Series history. Rivera appeared in seven Fall Classics with the Yankees, winning five of them. He saved three of the four Yankee victories in 1998. Then, in 1999, he didn't allow a single run in three appearances and was named the World Series MVP. Rivera has pitched in 24 World Series games, the most in history.

**World Series Stats**

| Games | Wins | Losses | Saves | ERA | Strikeouts |
|-------|------|--------|-------|------|------------|
| 24 | 2 | 1 | 11 | 0.99 | 32 |

## BABE RUTH

Babe Ruth was a pitcher for the Red Sox in his first two World Series. In 1916 and 1918, he went 3–0 with a 0.87 ERA to lead Boston to two titles. After the Red Sox traded him to the Yankees, Ruth became an outfielder. And he was even better! His finest series came in 1928. Ruth batted .625 and hit three homers in New York's four-game sweep of the Cardinals. His 15 World Series home runs remain the second most of all time.

**World Series Stats**

| Games | Avg. | HR | RBI | R |
|-------|------|-----|-----|-----|
| 41 | .326 | 15 | 33 | 37 |

Ruth hits a double in Game 1 of the 1928 World Series.

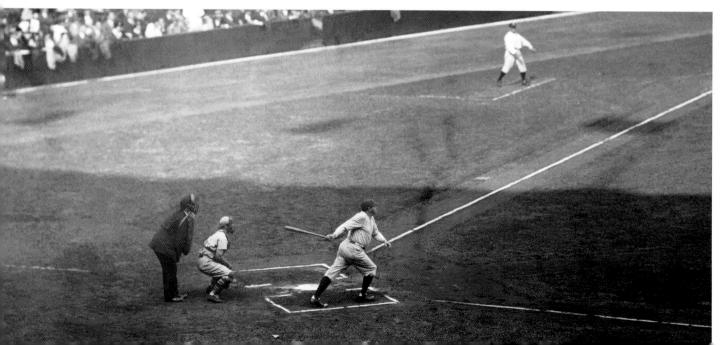

## PABLO SANDOVAL

Sandoval's first World Series appearance was bittersweet. His Giants won the championship, but he was hitless in three at-bats during the series.

His return to the series two years later was much more exciting. In Game 1, Sandoval—affectionately nicknamed Kung Fu Panda because of his portly build— became just the fourth player ever to hit three home runs in a World Series game. *(His third home run is pictured below.)* Two of those came off Detroit's Justin Verlander, the most dominant pitcher in baseball that season. In the Giants' sweep of the Tigers, Sandoval batted .500 and ran away with series MVP honors.

### World Series Stats

| Games | Avg. | HR | RBI | R |
|-------|------|----|-----|---|
| 5 | .421 | 3 | 4 | 3 |

# 4 FROM THE BLACK SOX TO THE BLOODY SOCK

## MEMORABLE WORLD SERIES MOMENTS

The World Series isn't just about great down-to-the-wire games. Sometimes it's a great individual feat, a strange play, or a majestic home run that sticks in fans' minds. From the unusual to the scandalous to the mind-boggling, here are some of the most memorable moments in World Series history.

### GAME EIGHT!
#### 1912, Game 8, Giants vs. Red Sox

That's not a typo—although the 1912 World Series was a best-of-seven contest, the series actually went to Game 8!

So what gives? In 1912 teams played only day games. Stadiums didn't have the lighting needed to play after sunset. That wasn't usually a problem. But by October, the days grow short. When Game 2 stretched into the 11th inning with the score tied at 6–6, it was too dark to keep playing. It was declared a tie. So when the Giants beat the Red Sox in Game 7 and each team had won three games, the series carried on. Game 8!

Game 8 was more than just a novelty—it was a heck of a game. Ace Christy Mathewson started for the Giants. He was brilliant, just as he had been all series. The score was 1–1 after nine innings. The Giants scored a run in the top of the 10th, and Mathewson came on to pitch the bottom half of the inning. Mathewson got the first batter to hit a pop fly, but outfielder Fred Snodgrass dropped it. Later in the inning, three Giants fielders converged on a pop foul, but none of them actually caught it. The Red Sox took advantage of the miscues, scoring two runs to win a one-of-a-kind game. Mathewson was the losing pitcher, despite one of the best World Series pitching performances in history!

## THE BLACK SOX SCANDAL
### 1919 World Series

Not all World Series moments are memorable for the right reasons. The 1919 World Series between the White Sox and the Reds remains one of the most talked about in history.

The White Sox sent star pitcher Eddie Cicotte to the mound for Game 1. With his second pitch, Cicotte drilled Cincinnati's Morrie Rath in the back. But this was no errant pitch. Cicotte was sending a message, not to the Reds but to a group of gamblers who had paid him and other members of the White Sox to throw the series. Since the Reds were heavy underdogs, the gamblers could make a fortune by betting big on them to win. When Cicotte hit Rath, it was the signal the gamblers were waiting for—he and his teammates were going to lose the World Series on purpose.

The beanball was just the beginning. Over the course of the seven-game series, eight players conspired to let the Reds win. Pitchers threw easy-to-hit fastballs down the middle of the plate. Fielders botched one play after the next. Batters didn't really try to get hits. But midway through the series, the gangsters who had set up the fix failed to deliver some of the promised payments to the players. So the players stopped losing on purpose. Chicago won three games. Needless to say, this did not please the gangsters who had bet heavily on the Reds. Under threat of violence, the "Black Sox" eventually finished their job of losing the series 5–3.

Rumors swirled about the fix, but it wasn't until the following season that the headlines came out. Fans were appalled at the news that the Fall Classic had been a farce. The players were charged with fraud. Despite several confessions, the jury found them not guilty. But new baseball commissioner Kenesaw Mountain Landis quickly let them know that they were not off the hook. He banned all eight players from baseball for life. He released the following statement:

> Regardless of the verdict of juries, no player that throws a ball game, no player that entertains proposals or promises to throw a game, no player that sits in a conference with a bunch of crooked players and gamblers where the ways and means of throwing games are discussed, and does not promptly tell his club about it, will ever play professional baseball.

## SHOELESS JOE

The most famous participant in the Black Sox scandal was Shoeless Joe Jackson. The star outfielder got his nickname as a teenager, playing semipro baseball. He had a new pair of shoes, but they gave him blisters. So one day, he took them off and went to bat in his socks.

Jackson was one of the game's great hitters. His .356 career batting average ranks third in the modern era. Had the Black Sox scandal never happened, he would stand as one of the game's all-time greats. Instead, his name stands as a black eye on the sport.

Jackson played the 1920 season as the investigation continued. He was brilliant as ever, batting .382, despite the distraction of the investigation. It would be his last season, however. Jackson admitted to taking money from the gamblers, although he insisted that he always played his best and did nothing to throw the games. And the numbers back up his claim. Jackson got a World Series-record 12 hits in the series and batted .375—hardly the numbers one would expect from someone trying to lose. His argument fell on deaf ears, however. He'd taken the money and tarnished the reputation of the game. That earned him a ban from the game—a ban that still stands, keeping the icon out of baseball's Hall of Fame.

## CAUGHT STEALING
### 1926, Game 7, Cardinals vs. Yankees

Babe Ruth is a baseball legend, one of the all-time great World Series performers. He was a great pitcher and baseball's first true power hitter. But Ruth's game was missing one thing: speed.

In 1926 the Yankees and Cardinals battled to a deciding Game 7. In the bottom of the ninth, the Cardinals were clinging to a 3–2 lead. Ruth stepped to the plate with two outs. St. Louis ace Grover Cleveland Alexander got ahead in the count, one ball and two strikes. Ruth was down to his last strike. But Alexander pitched the slugger carefully, not wanting to give him anything good to hit. Ruth was patient and drew a walk.

The portly Ruth trotted to first base. Outfielder Bob Meusel was up. Ruth knew that nobody would expect him to try to steal second. He took his lead off first and then darted toward second as soon as Alexander went into his windup. The move may have come as a surprise to the Cardinals. But that didn't change the fact that Ruth wasn't very fast. Meusel swung through the pitch. The ball popped into the mitt of catcher Bob O'Farrell, who stood and fired it down to second baseman Rogers Hornsby. Hornsby's tag beat Ruth to the bag. *Out!*

It remains the only World Series ever to end with a player caught stealing. And it stands as proof that Babe Ruth was indeed human.

Babe Ruth is tagged out at second base to end Game 7 of the 1926 World Series.

## THE BABE CALLS HIS SHOT
### 1932, Game 3, Yankees vs. Cubs

When most people think of Babe Ruth and the World Series, it's not his failed stolen base attempt they remember. It's the image of him pointing to the center-field bleachers during the fifth inning of Game 3 and then hitting a home run to that very spot.

Exactly what happened that day remains unclear. What we do know is that the Cubs' bench had been talking trash with Ruth that day. Ruth was never one to back down from a fight, so he was happy to give it right back to the Cubs. The friendly rivalry continued when Ruth came to bat in the fifth inning. When Cubs' pitcher Charlie Root got strike one, Ruth raised his right hand and put up one finger. When Root got a second strike, Ruth did it again, this time putting up two fingers. Ruth then shouted something at Root and pointed to center field. He belted the next pitch over the center-field fence.

Legend tells that Ruth called his shot. After the game, Ruth denied it. He said that he was just pointing to the Chicago dugout. But later in life, Ruth changed his story, claiming that he really did call his shot. The debate over what really happened lives on, and it's unlikely we'll ever know for sure.

## SLAUGHTER'S MAD DASH
### 1946, Game 7, Cardinals vs. Red Sox

In 1946 the Cardinals and the Red Sox squared off in a classic World Series. The series went to a deciding seventh game, and the score was tied 3–3 in the eighth inning. All-Star outfield Enos Slaughter led off the bottom of the eighth for St. Louis with a solid single. But neither of the next two batters could advance him to second base.

With two outs, outfielder Harry Walker stepped to the plate. Walker lined the ball to left-center field. Slaughter was running as soon as the ball was hit. He sped past second base as Boston center fielder Leon Culberson briefly bobbled the ball and then threw to second baseman Johnny Pesky.

The Cardinals' third-base coach gave Slaughter the stop sign, but Slaughter ignored it. He tore around third base at full speed. Pesky appeared surprised to see the runner trying to score. He hesitated for a split second before throwing home. His throw was weak and off target, and Slaughter slid into home with the series-winning run *(right)*. "Slaughter's Mad Dash" was proof that a player could change a game—and a World Series—with his legs as well as his bat.

## COOKIE BREAKS IT UP
### 1947, Game 4, Yankees vs. Dodgers

Yankee pitcher Bill Bevens was on the verge of making history in Game 4 of the 1947 World Series. He stood on the mound just one out from throwing the first no-hitter in World Series history. Bevens was far from perfect that day. He'd walked 10 batters and had allowed a run. But he hadn't allowed a hit, and he was nursing a 2–1 lead over the Dodgers.

With two runners on, Brooklyn sent pinch hitter Cookie Lavagetto to the plate. Bevens delivered to Lavagetto, who drilled a single to right field. Both runners came around to score. On one pitch, Bevens had lost the no-hitter *and* the game! Bevens

The Brooklyn Dodgers lift team hero Cookie Lavagetto onto their shoulders following his game-winning hit in the 1947 World Series.

and the Yankees did get the last laugh, however, beating the Dodgers in seven games.

### THE CATCH
### 1954, Game 1,
### Giants vs. Indians

Say the name Willie Mays to almost any hard-core baseball fan, and they'll think of one play. It happened in the first game of the 1954 World Series, as Mays's New York Giants faced off against the Cleveland Indians.

The score was tied, 2–2, in the eighth inning. Cleveland was rallying, with two runners on and one out. Vic Wertz stepped to the plate. Wertz was a power hitter, but the Giants had Don Liddle on the mound, and Liddle was known for getting opposing batters to hit ground balls. So Mays was playing a very shallow center field.

Liddle delivered a pitch, and Wertz launched it high and far. It looked like a sure extra-base hit that would score the runners. But Mays turned and sprinted toward the fence. With his back to home plate, he caught the ball over his shoulder. Then he turned, and in one motion, he fired the ball to second base, preventing one of the runners from tagging up and advancing a base.

Willie Mays makes the catch and throws the ball to second in a single rapid movement during Game 1 of the 1954 World Series.

Everyone was stunned. Nobody had ever seen anything like it. Mays always insisted that the catch was nothing special. But fans, coaches, and Mays's fellow players knew better. It remains perhaps the most famous defensive play in baseball history.

## PERFECTION
## 1956, Game 5,
## Yankees vs. Dodgers

One of the rarest achievements in baseball is the perfect game. A pitcher must retire every man he faces. No hits, no walks, and no errors. No base runners for any reason. Perfection. It has only happened 21 times in baseball's modern era. The most famous perfect game in history came on baseball's biggest stage.

New York Yankee Don Larsen hardly seemed like the man who would pitch the only perfect game in World Series history. In 1956 he spent time as a starter and a reliever. He was not known as a dominating pitcher. He had started Game 2 of the series and hadn't lasted even two innings. When he made his next start in Game 5, the result was quite different.

Don Larsen pitches the top of the eighth inning during Game 5 of the 1956 World Series. His is the only perfect game pitched in the history of the World Series.

Larsen seemed like a different pitcher on the mound. The same team that had battered him a few days before looked lost against him. He threw his 97th—and final—pitch to pinch hitter Dale Mitchell. Mitchell watched strike three whiz by. Larsen had done it! The Yankees mobbed him on the mound. Perfection in the World Series—it's an accomplishment that may never be matched.

## POLISHING OFF THE UPSET
### 1969, Game 5, Orioles vs. Mets

The 1969 Baltimore Orioles were a powerhouse. Their 109–53 record was the best in baseball that season. They dominated during the regular season and crushed the Minnesota Twins in the American League Championship Series (ALCS). Meanwhile, the surprisingly successful New York Mets won the NL pennant.

Most expected the Orioles to easily dispatch the Mets. But the Miracle Mets had spent the whole season exceeding expectations. They were ready to do it one more time. New York jumped out to a 3–1 series lead. Game 5, in New York, gave them a chance to complete their miracle season.

Baltimore led 3–0 when the Mets came to bat in the bottom of the sixth. Dave McNally threw a pitch toward the feet of hitter Cleon Jones. The ball bounced toward the New York dugout. The umpire ruled that the ball had hit the dirt. But Mets' manager Gil Hodges charged out onto the field, ball in hand. Hodges showed the home plate umpire a spot of shoe polish on the ball—proof that it had indeed hit Jones in the foot. Jones was awarded first base, and the Mets went on to rally for two runs in the inning. They completed the comeback and won the game, 5–3. And if not for a bit of shoe polish, it might never have happened.

## BUCKNER!
### 1986, Game 6, Red Sox vs. Mets

In 1986 the Red Sox appeared on the verge of breaking one of the longest championship droughts in baseball history (they had not won a title since 1918). They led the New York Mets in the series 3–2, and in Game 6, they took a 5–3 lead in the top of the 10th inning.

Boston first baseman Bill Buckner was playing the series on aching knees. The Red Sox had replaced him in the late innings of several earlier games in the series, opting for a more capable defensive player. But in Game 6, manager John McNamara stuck with Buckner.

Boston relief pitcher Calvin Schiraldi retired the first two batters in the bottom of the 10th. The Red Sox were one out away from a championship. But the next two hitters got singles.

New York's Ray Knight stepped to the plate. He swung and missed at two pitches. Boston was a single strike away from victory. But then Knight got a single of his

own, driving in a run. It was 5–4 Boston. The Red Sox put reliever Bob Stanley into the game. Stanley threw a wild pitch that allowed the tying run to score. Then he got Mookie Wilson to hit a weak ground ball to first base.

Buckner needed only to field the ball and step on first to send the game to the 11th inning. But he rushed the play, and the ball rolled between his legs *(left)*. Knight ran home, holding his head in disbelief, to score the winning run. The Mets went on to win Game 7 and the series. That moment haunts Red Sox fans to this day.

## GIBSON'S BIG SHOT
### 1988, Game 1, A's vs. Dodgers

The situation looked bleak for the Los Angeles Dodgers in Game 1 of the 1988 World Series. They trailed 4–3. Oakland A's closer Dennis Eckersley was on the mound. With his unusual windup and blazing fastball, Eck was the game's most dominating closer. He was as close to automatic as it got.

Eckersley got two quick outs. Pinch hitter Mike Davis stood at the plate. Davis had power, so the A's wanted to pitch him carefully. In addition, Dodger manager Tommy Lasorda had sent the weak-hitting Dave Anderson into the on-deck circle. Eckersley gave Davis little to hit in the strike zone and ended up walking him.

But Lasorda had a trick up his sleeve. Slugger Kirk Gibson had been out with an injured leg. Gibson couldn't run, but he assured Lasorda that he could swing the bat. And so Gibson, not Anderson, limped up to home plate.

It was a big gamble. Gibson couldn't run, so he'd be out if he hit almost anything on the ground. With a full count, Eckersley delivered a slider. Gibson was expecting it. He hacked with all his might. It was an awkward, unusual, one-legged swing. But Gibson's strength was enough. The ball jumped off his bat and soared way out to the right-field seats. Gibson pumped his arm as he slowly rounded the bases *(right)*, and Dodger fans celebrated one of the most memorable home runs in baseball history.

## EARTHMOVER
### 1989, Prior to Game 3, A's vs. Giants

The 1989 World Series became known as the Battle of the Bay, as the teams from Oakland and San Francisco—cities just across San Francisco Bay from each other—faced off. The action on the field was somewhat unremarkable, with Oakland sweeping the Giants in four games. What most baseball fans remember about the series had nothing to do with baseball.

Game 3 was scheduled to begin at Candlestick Park in San Francisco at 5:35 local time on October 17. At 5:04, the stadium was filling. Players were warming up. Television and radio broadcasters were doing their pregame shows. Then the earth began to shake.

The 7.1-magnitude earthquake lasted 15 seconds, knocking out power all over the area, damaging buildings, and collapsing many highways. A total of 63 people died as a result of the quake, though everyone at the stadium was fine. Officials later said that the timing of the game may have saved lives. Many people in the area had left work early to be home in time for the first pitch, meaning there were fewer cars on the highways that collapsed. And the cameras aboard a blimp flying above the stadium to provide aerial coverage of the game helped officials assess the damage to the city and respond quickly.

The game was delayed 10 days. It was finally played October 27, with the A's winning 13–7. Firefighters and police officers who had been among the first responders during the earthquake were honored before the game by throwing out the ceremonial first pitch.

## CLIMB ON MY BACK
### 1991, Game 6, Braves vs. Twins

The Minnesota Twins found themselves down 3–2 in the 1991 World Series. But superstar outfielder Kirby Puckett wasn't worried. According to reports, before Game 6, Puckett spoke to his teammates. He told them to climb on his back, promising to carry them to a deciding Game 7.

It wasn't idle talk. In the third inning, with a runner on first, Atlanta's Ron Gant hit a deep fly ball to center. Puckett tracked it, leaped just in front of the fence, and made an amazing catch, robbing Gant of an extra-base hit and preventing a run from scoring.

The game went to extra innings. Puckett came to the plate in the bottom of the 11th with the score tied 3–3. He took the first three pitches from Charlie Leibrandt. On the fourth pitch, Puckett launched a game-winning home run to left-center field, delivering on his promise. In addition to his big catch, Puckett went 3–4 and drove in three runs to set up Game 7, which the Twins also won in dramatic fashion.

Kirby Puckett *(center)* and his Minnesota Twins teammates celebrate winning the 1991 World Series.

## THE BLOODY SOCK
### 2004, Game 2, Cardinals vs. Red Sox

The Boston Red Sox reached the 2004 World Series after an amazing comeback in the ALCS. The Red Sox trailed the Yankees 3–0 in the ALCS before winning four in a row to advance to the World Series. Starting pitcher Curt Schilling suffered a torn tendon in his ankle during that ALCS but refused to rest.

Schilling took the mound in Game 2 of the World Series against the Cardinals, despite having had stitches in his ankle just the day before. During the game, TV cameras zoomed in on Schilling's injured ankle, showing a prominent bloody spot *(right)* on his sock.

## THE CURSE OF THE BAMBINO

Babe Ruth and the Red Sox won the World Series in 1918. The Red Sox sold Ruth to the Yankees the following year. Ruth went on to make the Yankees the most successful team in baseball history, while the fate of the Red Sox went the opposite direction for decades.

Fans in Boston came to believe that the franchise was cursed and that it had been since the moment Ruth was sold to the Yankees. When Bill Buckner let a ground ball trickle through his legs in 1986, some fans were furious with him. Others just chalked it up to the curse. The Red Sox appeared cursed again in 2004 when the Yankees jumped out to a 3–0 lead in the ALCS. But the curse apparently ended there. The Red Sox won their next eight games—four to beat the Yankees and four to sweep the Cardinals in the World Series—and the curse was over.

In a performance that some called heroic, Schilling threw six innings, allowing just one unearned run, and got the win for the Sox. Boston went on to sweep the series, their first championship since 1918.

## ONE-MAN WRECKING CREW 2011, Game 3, Cardinals vs. Rangers

The first two games of the 2011 World Series between the Rangers and the Cardinals hadn't produced much offense. The teams had combined for just eight runs. St. Louis fans and the media had begun to grumble about the lack of big hits from the Cardinals' Albert Pujols, widely regarded as the greatest hitter of his generation. Pujols, who had struggled in past World Series, was 0–6 in the first two games.

In Game 3, he answered his critics with what may have been the most amazing individual hitting performance in World Series history. It actually started with an out. In the first inning, Pujols smashed a line drive toward third base. But the slick-fielding Adrian Beltre snared it to rob Pujols of a hit. It was the only time the Rangers would get Prince Albert out that night. He singled in the fourth inning and then again in the fifth. He stepped to the plate in the sixth inning with two runners on and blasted a big three-run homer.

Pujols homered again in the seventh inning, this time a two-run shot. By the ninth inning, the Cardinals led 15–7. With the game being played in Texas, many disgusted Ranger fans had left early, leaving the stadium only about half full. Those who left missed a chance to witness history. Pujols got one more at bat, and he took advantage of it. His solo home run was his third of the game. Only Babe Ruth and Reggie Jackson had ever hit that many home runs in a World Series game. (San Francisco's Pablo Sandoval matched the feat the following year.) Pujols also tied World Series records with five hits and six RBIs in a game.

Albert Pujols hits his third home run of Game 3 in the 2011 World Series.

Reporters and fans spend endless hours writing about and debating the present—and future—of baseball. According to some, it's all doom and gloom. Baseball once earned the nickname America's Pastime. But now, professional football is by far the most popular spectator sport in the United States. Baseball is an old man's game, some argue. Younger sports fans are drawn to the fast-paced, star-driven action of professional basketball, auto racing, or action sports.

Yet, if this is true, it isn't showing up on the bottom line for Major League Baseball owners—or players. The sport brings in more than $7 billion each year. By comparison, that number hovered just over $1 billion in 1992. The sport's popularity has exploded in Latin America and throughout much of eastern Asia, opening up new markets and a broader talent pool. If anything, baseball seems to be getting stronger, despite recent dramas of work stoppages and steroid scandals.

## CONTINUING TRADITION

While baseball's regular season and playoffs have gone through many changes in recent decades, the formula for the World Series has remained mostly constant. Aside

The San Francisco Giants celebrate winning the 2012 World Series.

from a change in 2003 to award home-field advantage to the league that wins the All-Star Game, the World Series format has been mostly untouched for decades. Baseball fans, perhaps more than fans of any other major team sport, value tradition. It's for that reason that baseball is unlikely to tinker with a winning format anytime soon.

Of course, controversy will never go away. As baseball continues to expand its playoff format, one can envision a scenario in which one or more teams with losing regular-season records get into the playoffs. Should such a team get hot and make it to the Fall Classic, the outcry from baseball purists would be inevitable. But it's a possibility that leagues such as the National Football League, the National Basketball Association, and the National Hockey League have lived with for years, and those leagues continue to grow and thrive. There's no reason to believe baseball would be any different.

It's hard to imagine what baseball and the World Series might look like in 30, 50, or even 100 years. Franchises will move. Rivalries will shift. Rules will change. But it seems likely that baseball's ultimate stage will look much as it does today—and much as it did 100 years ago.

# WORLD SERIES RESULTS

| SEASON | WINNER | LOSER | SERIES |
|---|---|---|---|
| 2012 | San Francisco Giants | Detroit Tigers | 4–0 |
| 2011 | St. Louis Cardinals | Texas Rangers | 4–3 |
| 2010 | San Francisco Giants | Texas Rangers | 4–1 |
| 2009 | New York Yankees | Philadelphia Phillies | 4–2 |
| 2008 | Philadelphia Phillies | Tampa Bay Rays | 4–1 |
| 2007 | Boston Red Sox | Colorado Rockies | 4–0 |
| 2006 | St. Louis Cardinals | Detroit Tigers | 4–1 |
| 2005 | Chicago White Sox | Houston Astros | 4–0 |
| 2004 | Boston Red Sox | St. Louis Cardinals | 4–0 |
| 2003 | Florida Marlins | New York Yankees | 4–2 |
| 2002 | Anaheim Angels | San Francisco Giants | 4–3 |
| 2001 | Arizona Diamondbacks | New York Yankees | 4–3 |
| 2000 | New York Yankees | New York Mets | 4–1 |
| 1999 | New York Yankees | Atlanta Braves | 4–0 |
| 1998 | New York Yankees | San Diego Padres | 4–0 |
| 1997 | Florida Marlins | Cleveland Indians | 4–3 |
| 1996 | New York Yankees | Atlanta Braves | 4–2 |
| 1995 | Atlanta Braves | Cleveland Indians | 4–2 |
| 1993 | Toronto Blue Jays | Philadelphia Phillies | 4–2 |
| 1992 | Toronto Blue Jays | Atlanta Braves | 4–2 |
| 1991 | Minnesota Twins | Atlanta Braves | 4–3 |
| 1990 | Cincinnati Reds | Oakland Athletics | 4–0 |
| 1989 | Oakland Athletics | San Francisco Giants | 4–0 |
| 1988 | Los Angeles Dodgers | Oakland Athletics | 4–1 |
| 1987 | Minnesota Twins | St. Louis Cardinals | 4–3 |
| 1986 | New York Mets | Boston Red Sox | 4–3 |
| 1985 | Kansas City Royals | St. Louis Cardinals | 4–3 |
| 1984 | Detroit Tigers | San Diego Padres | 4–1 |
| 1983 | Baltimore Orioles | Philadelphia Phillies | 4–1 |
| 1982 | St. Louis Cardinals | Milwaukee Brewers | 4–3 |
| 1981 | Los Angeles Dodgers | New York Yankees | 4–2 |
| 1980 | Philadelphia Phillies | Kansas City Royals | 4–2 |
| 1979 | Pittsburgh Pirates | Baltimore Orioles | 4–3 |
| 1978 | New York Yankees | Los Angeles Dodgers | 4–2 |
| 1977 | New York Yankees | Los Angeles Dodgers | 4–2 |
| 1976 | Cincinnati Reds | New York Yankees | 4–0 |
| 1975 | Cincinnati Reds | Boston Red Sox | 4–3 |
| 1974 | Oakland Athletics | Los Angeles Dodgers | 4–1 |
| 1973 | Oakland Athletics | New York Mets | 4–3 |
| 1972 | Oakland Athletics | Cincinnati Reds | 4–3 |
| 1971 | Pittsburgh Pirates | Baltimore Orioles | 4–3 |
| 1970 | Baltimore Orioles | Cincinnati Reds | 4–1 |
| 1969 | New York Mets | Baltimore Orioles | 4–1 |
| 1968 | Detroit Tigers | St. Louis Cardinals | 4–3 |
| 1967 | St. Louis Cardinals | Boston Red Sox | 4–3 |
| 1966 | Baltimore Orioles | Los Angeles Dodgers | 4–0 |
| 1965 | Los Angeles Dodgers | Minnesota Twins | 4–3 |
| 1964 | St. Louis Cardinals | New York Yankees | 4–3 |
| 1963 | Los Angeles Dodgers | New York Yankees | 4–0 |
| 1962 | New York Yankees | San Francisco Giants | 4–3 |
| 1961 | New York Yankees | Cincinnati Reds | 4–1 |
| 1960 | Pittsburgh Pirates | New York Yankees | 4–3 |
| 1959 | Los Angeles Dodgers | Chicago White Sox | 4–2 |
| 1958 | New York Yankees | Milwaukee Braves | 4–3 |

| SEASON | WINNER | LOSER | SERIES |
|--------|--------|-------|--------|
| 1957 | Milwaukee Braves | New York Yankees | 4–3 |
| 1956 | New York Yankees | Brooklyn Dodgers | 4–3 |
| 1955 | Brooklyn Dodgers | New York Yankees | 4–3 |
| 1954 | New York Giants | Cleveland Indians | 4–0 |
| 1953 | New York Yankees | Brooklyn Dodgers | 4–2 |
| 1952 | New York Yankees | Brooklyn Dodgers | 4–3 |
| 1951 | New York Yankees | New York Giants | 4–2 |
| 1950 | New York Yankees | Philadelphia Phillies | 4–0 |
| 1949 | New York Yankees | Brooklyn Dodgers | 4–1 |
| 1948 | Cleveland Indians | Boston Braves | 4–2 |
| 1947 | New York Yankees | Brooklyn Dodgers | 4–3 |
| 1946 | St. Louis Cardinals | Boston Red Sox | 4–3 |
| 1945 | Detroit Tigers | Chicago Cubs | 4–3 |
| 1944 | St. Louis Cardinals | St. Louis Browns | 4–2 |
| 1943 | New York Yankees | St. Louis Cardinals | 4–1 |
| 1942 | St. Louis Cardinals | New York Yankees | 4–1 |
| 1941 | New York Yankees | Brooklyn Dodgers | 4–1 |
| 1940 | Cincinnati Reds | Detroit Tigers | 4–3 |
| 1939 | New York Yankees | Cincinnati Reds | 4–0 |
| 1938 | New York Yankees | Chicago Cubs | 4–0 |
| 1937 | New York Yankees | New York Giants | 4–1 |
| 1936 | New York Yankees | New York Giants | 4–2 |
| 1935 | Detroit Tigers | Chicago Cubs | 4–2 |
| 1934 | St. Louis Cardinals | Detroit Tigers | 4–3 |
| 1933 | New York Giants | Washington Nationals | 4–1 |
| 1932 | New York Yankees | Chicago Cubs | 4–0 |
| 1931 | St. Louis Cardinals | Philadelphia Athletics | 4–3 |
| 1930 | Philadelphia Athletics | St. Louis Cardinals | 4–2 |
| 1929 | Philadelphia Athletics | Chicago Cubs | 4–1 |
| 1928 | New York Yankees | St. Louis Cardinals | 4–0 |
| 1927 | New York Yankees | Pittsburgh Pirates | 4–0 |
| 1926 | St. Louis Cardinals | New York Yankees | 4–3 |
| 1925 | Pittsburgh Pirates | Washington Nationals | 4–3 |
| 1924 | Washington Nationals | New York Giants | 4–3 |
| 1923 | New York Yankees | New York Giants | 4–2 |
| 1922 | New York Giants | New York Yankees | 4–0 |
| 1921 | New York Giants | New York Yankees | 5–3 |
| 1920 | Cleveland Indians | Brooklyn Robins | 5–2 |
| 1919 | Cincinnati Reds | Chicago White Sox | 5–3 |
| 1918 | Boston Red Sox | Chicago Cubs | 4–2 |
| 1917 | Chicago White Sox | New York Giants | 4–2 |
| 1916 | Boston Red Sox | Brooklyn Robins | 4–1 |
| 1915 | Boston Red Sox | Philadelphia Phillies | 4–1 |
| 1914 | Boston Braves | Philadelphia Athletics | 4–0 |
| 1913 | Philadelphia Athletics | New York Giants | 4–1 |
| 1912 | Boston Red Sox | New York Giants | 4–3 |
| 1911 | Philadelphia Athletics | New York Giants | 4–2 |
| 1910 | Philadelphia Athletics | Chicago Cubs | 4–1 |
| 1909 | Pittsburgh Pirates | Detroit Tigers | 4–3 |
| 1908 | Chicago Cubs | Detroit Tigers | 4–1 |
| 1907 | Chicago Cubs | Detroit Tigers | 4–0 |
| 1906 | Chicago White Sox | Chicago Cubs | 4–2 |
| 1905 | New York Giants | Philadelphia Athletics | 4–1 |
| 1903 | Boston Americans | Pittsburgh Pirates | 5–3 |

# SOURCE NOTES

27 Rick Weinburg, "43: Joe Carter's Home Run Wins 1993 World Series," *ESPN.com*, accessed April 8, 2013, http://sports.espn.go.com/espn/espn25/story?page=moments/43.

31 Gene Wojciechowski, "Game 6 Delivers a True Fall Classic," *ESPN.com*, October 28, 2011, http://sports.espn.go.com/espn/columns/story?columnist=wojciechowski_gene&page=wojciechowski-111027&sportCat=mlb.

44 "1919 World Series," *Baseball Almanac*, accessed August 2, 2013, http://www.baseball-almanac.com/ws/yr1919ws.shtml.

# GLOSSARY

**ace:** a team's best starting pitcher

**favorite:** a team expected by most to win a game or a series

**gangster:** a member of an organized group of criminals

**revenue:** income generated by a company or an organization

**sweep:** a series in which one team wins all the games played

**underdog:** a team expected by most to lose a game or a series

**upset:** a game or a series in which a heavy underdog wins

**walk-off:** a play in which a home team scores a run in the bottom of the ninth (or extra innings) to end the game

# FURTHER READING

## Books

Buckley, James. *Baseball.* New York: DK Publishing, 2010.

Doeden, Matt. *Willie Mays.* Minneapolis: Twenty-First Century Books, 2011.

Fischer, David. *Babe Ruth: Legendary Slugger.* New York: Sterling, 2010.

Fishman, Jon. *Mariano Rivera.* Minneapolis: Lerner Publications, 2014.

Hardman, Lizabeth. *Baseball.* Detroit: Lucent Books, 2011.

Hoblin, Paul. *Great Hitters of the Negro Leagues.* Minneapolis: Abdo Pub. Company, 2013.

Marlin, John. *Mickey Mantle.* Minneapolis: Twenty-First Century Books, 2005.

Stewart, Mark, and Mike Kennedy. *Long Ball: The Legend and Lore of the Home Run.* Minneapolis: Millbrook Press, 2006.

## Websites

**Baseball Almanac**                    **http://www.baseball-almanac.com**

Learn more about all things baseball at this site, with detailed descriptions of every World Series, bios of key players, and lots of stats.

**Baseball Reference**                   **http://www.baseball-reference.com**

Baseball Reference is the place to go for fans who love detailed stats and a century's worth of box scores.

**Major League Baseball**                **http://mlb.mlb.com**

Get the latest on your favorite MLB teams and players at the official site of Major League Baseball.

# INDEX

# ABOUT THE AUTHOR

Matt Doeden began his career as a sports writer. Since then, he's spent more than a decade writing and editing children's nonfiction, with more than 100 titles to his name. His titles *Sandy Koufax* and *Tom Brady: Unlikely Champion* were Junior Library Guild selections. Doeden lives in Minnesota with his wife and two children.

## Photo Acknowledgments

The images in this book are used with the permission of: © Dilip Vishwanat/Getty Images, p. 4–5; © Mark Rucker/Transcendental Graphics/Getty Images, p. 6; © Transcendental Graphics/Getty Images, p. 9; Underwood & Underwood/Wikimedia Commons, p. 11; © Bettmann/CORBIS, pp. 12, 19, 21, 33 (top and bottom), 40, 47, 50; © American Stock Archive/Getty Images, p. 13; © Jerry Coli/Dreamstime.com, p. 14; AP Photo/Hans Deryk, p. 15; © Ezra Shaw/Getty Images, p. 16; AP Photo/National Baseball Hall of Fame, Cooperstown, p. 17; © Daniel Raustadt/Dreamstime.com, p. 22; AP Photo/Harry Cabluck, p. 23; AP Photo/Mark Duncan, File, p. 25; © Ron Vesely/MLB Photos via Getty Images, p. 27; © MATT YORK/AFP/Getty Images, p. 28; © MIKE NELSON/AFP/Getty Images, p. 29; © Doug Pensinger/Getty Images, p. 31; © Underwood & Underwood/CORBIS, p. 34 (top); AP Photo, pp. 34 (bottom), 35; © Focus On Sport/Getty Images, pp. 36 (top and bottom); © Art Rickerby/Time Life Pictures/Getty Images, p. 37 (top); © FPG/Getty Images, p. 37 (bottom); © Rick Stewart/Getty Images, p. 38; AP Photo/Jim Mone, p. 39 (top); AP Photo/Ron Frehm, p. 39 (bottom); AP Photo/Jeff Chiu, p. 41; National Baseball Hall of Fame Library, Cooperstown, N.Y., p. 45; © Bill Meurer/NY Daily News Archive via Getty Images, p. 48; © NY Daily News Archive via Getty Images, p. 49; © Stan Grossfeld/The Boston Globe via Getty Imagess, p. 52; AP Photo/Rusty Kennedy, p. 53; © Brian Peterson/Minneapolis Star/ZUMA/CORBIS, p. 55 (top); © RAY STUBBLEBINE/Reuters/Corbis, p. 55 (bottom); © Rob Carr/Getty Images, p. 57; © Jonathan Daniel/Getty Images, p. 59.

Front Cover: © Thearon W. Henderson/Getty Images.
Jacket Flap: © Doug Pensinger/Getty Images (top), © Bettman/CORBIS (bottom).

Main body text set in Adobe Garamond Pro Regular 14/19.
Typeface provided by Adobe Systems.